ROBERT'S REAL ESTATE GAME!

By: **Dre Mudaris**
Illustrator By: **Cameron Wilson**

ISBN: 9798530240157

Copyright © 2021 Children To Wealth

All rights reserved.

ROBERT'S REAL ESTATE GAME

WRITTEN BY DRE MUDARIS
ILLUSTRATED BY CAMERON WILSON

All rights reserved.

Reading Levels

Interest Level: K-Gr. 7 DRA Level: 24 Lexile Measure: 770L

Grade Equivalent: 3.7 Guided Reading: M

WATCH ALONG
(SCAN CODE BELOW)

"I'm not liking this game at all," Robert says.

"Of course, you don't. I wouldn't like it either if I kept on losing." Cynthia says as the crowd at the table begins to laugh.

"Yeah yeah, whatever. This game always seems so fake." Robert says in disappointment.

"I win!" Jacob says with excitement.

5

"Nice, Jacob. Let's count how much we all have," Cynthia says.

"Um, you guys have fun. I see my parents are here. I have to go." Robert says as he gets up upon noticing his parent's car drive up.

Robert runs from the table to wait for his parents to check him out of the after-school program.

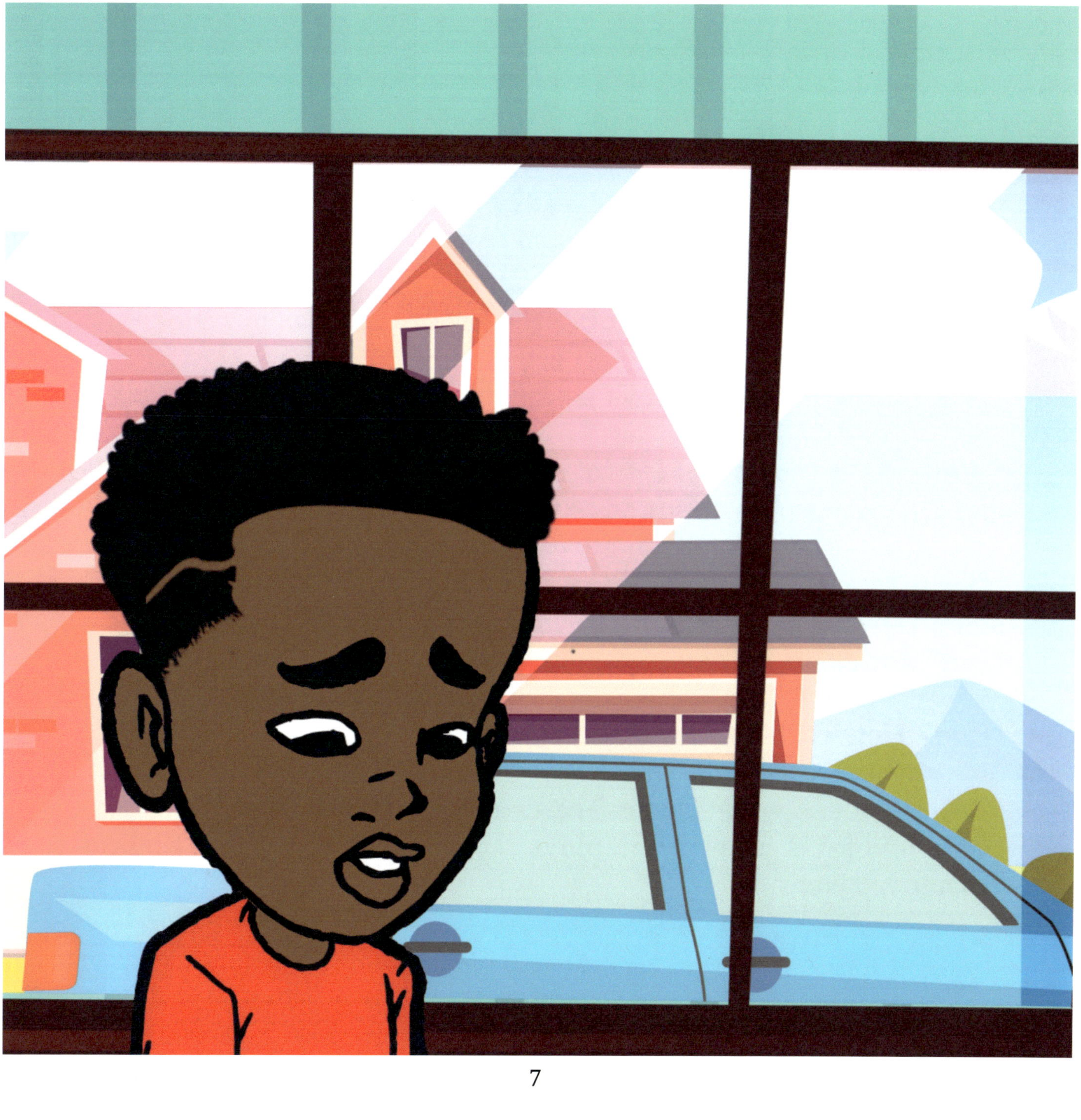

While in the car, Robert's parents can notice the sadness on Robert's face from the rearview mirror.

"What's wrong, champ?" Robert's father asks with concern.

"It's nothing," Robert says at first.

"Well... It's that stupid 'real estate game.' I don't understand it, and I never win!" Robert says with disappointment.

"Don't be upset, champ. That game can be tricky. It took me some time to learn it until I started working with your Uncle Dre." Robert's father says.

"Dad? How so?" Robert asks.

"Well, you see, your Uncle Dre created a real estate firm a while back, and let's just say he plays Monopoly in real life." Robert's father answers.

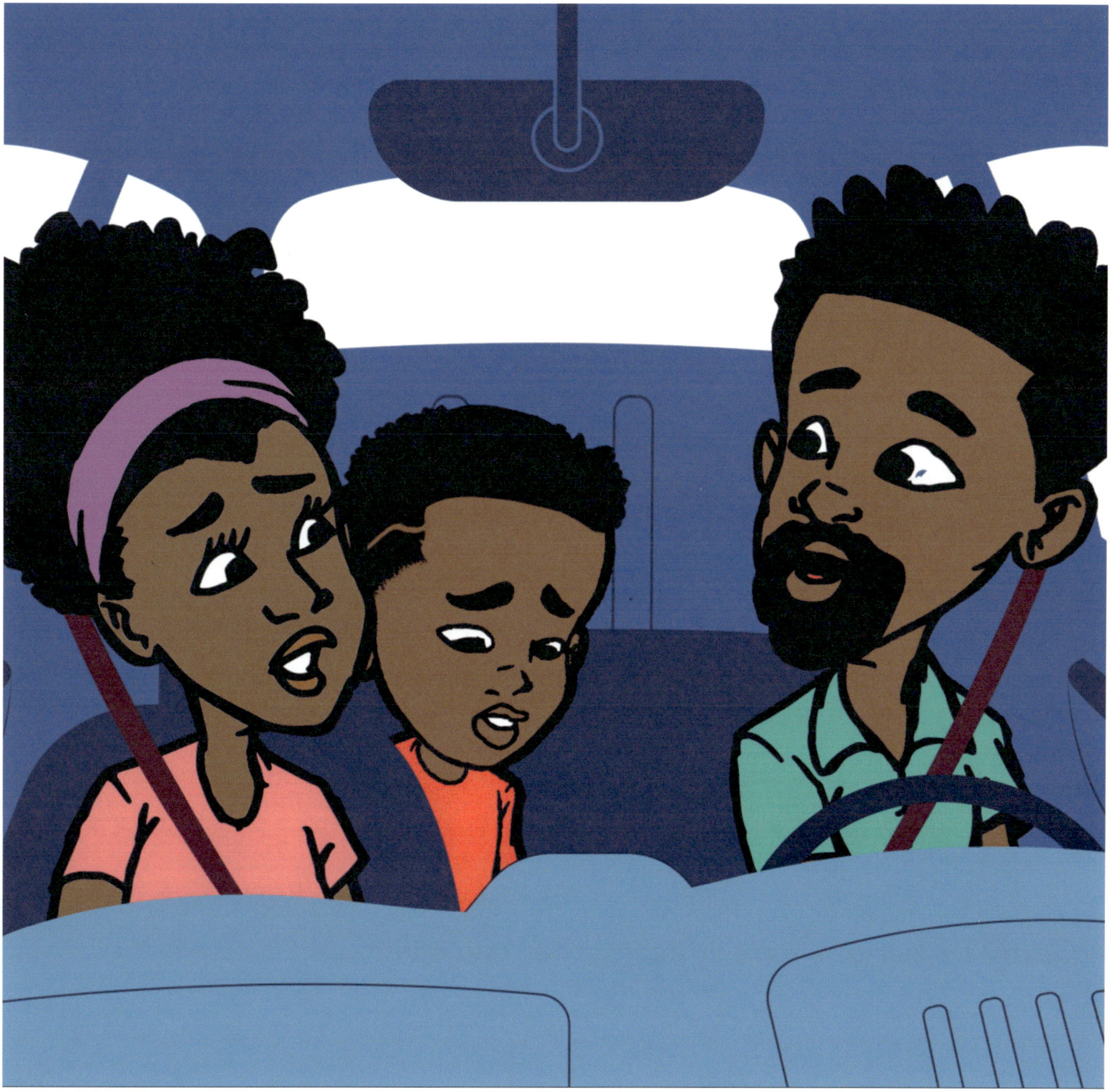

"I have an idea." Robert's mom interjects.

"Why don't you go out in the field with your Dad tomorrow instead of watching your Saturday morning cartoon shows." Robert's mom adds.

"Um, Ok," Robert says.

"That is a wonderful idea, honey. And Robert guess what? Uncle Dre flies in tomorrow morning. We will evaluate a few properties and see if they will be a good addition to our portfolio." Robert's dad says.

Robert's face lights up. He thinks of the "Real Estate Game." that he just lost in after school. And he then imagines himself winning the game, and he sees the reaction of all his classmates cheering him on instead of the previous thought of them laughing at him.

"Yay. I can't wait! Finally, I will learn this game and be able to win!" Robert says in excitement.

Robert's parents look at each other and smile.

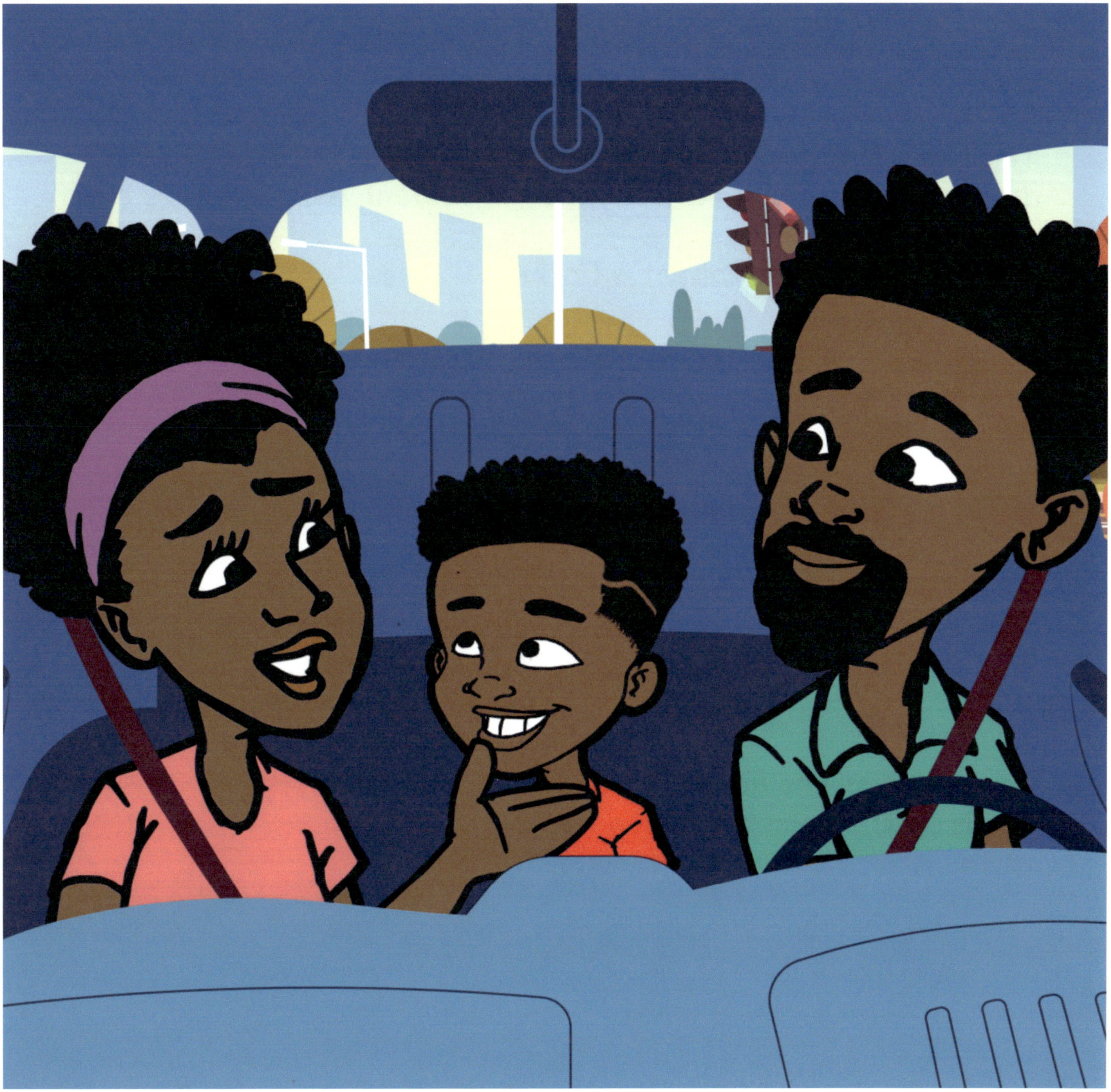

The Next Day, Robert is up bright and early, excited for the day ahead. Robert's Father yells for Robert from upstairs.

"Robert? Robert?" Robert's Father.

"Hey, Dad, I'm downstairs," Robert responds. Robert's Father walks downstairs and sees Robert at the kitchen table eating cereal while reading the back of the cereal box.

"I didn't expect you to be up this early." Robert's Father says. Before Robert can respond, the doorbell rings.

"I'm glad you're up. Finish your breakfast and grab your jacket. We are going to be heading out. That's your Uncle Dre." Robert's Father says.

Robert takes one more bite and rushes to grab his jacket, and heads to the door to meet with his Father in time. As he opens up the door for Uncle Dre.

13

"Good Morning, Fellas." Uncle Dre says.

"Good Morning Uncle Dre," Robert Says as he greets Uncle Dre.

"I hope you're ready for today! I sure have a lot to teach you today on Real Estate." Uncle Dre Says.

Robert Looks at his father and smiles. "Yes, I am!" Robert responds.

"Ok, Great. I'm going to take you for a ride-along today, and you will get to view some of my real estate projects in real-time and I will explain everything I can to you." Uncle Dre says.

"Perfect! I'm already dressed, and I had my breakfast! I'll meet you at the car." Robert says as he races out.

"Boy, is he excited?" Robert's Father Says.

"I would be too. We Should be back by 4'oclock" Uncle Dre says as he and Robert's Father walks to the car.

15

While Driving to Uncle Dre's current real estate projects, UncleDre asks Robert, "So what do you know so far."

"So far, you need to find a property, make it look nice, and then sell it," Robert responds.

"Simply put, you have the gist of it, and that is what your father and I do regularly, but there are many components and avenues to the Real Estate Game." Uncle Dre Responds.

"I like to think there are four ways to play and enter into the real estate game. They are wholesaling, fix and flip, buy and hold, and my favorite, the B.R.R.R.R strategy." Uncle Dre continues.

"What does B.R.R.R.R stand for?" Robert asks.

"Well, B is for Buy. The first R is for Renovate. The Second R is for renting the property out to a tenant. The third R is when you Refinance the property back to the bank. And the Last R stands for Repeat." Uncle Dre answers.

"Oh! I see. I like those acronyms." Robert responds.

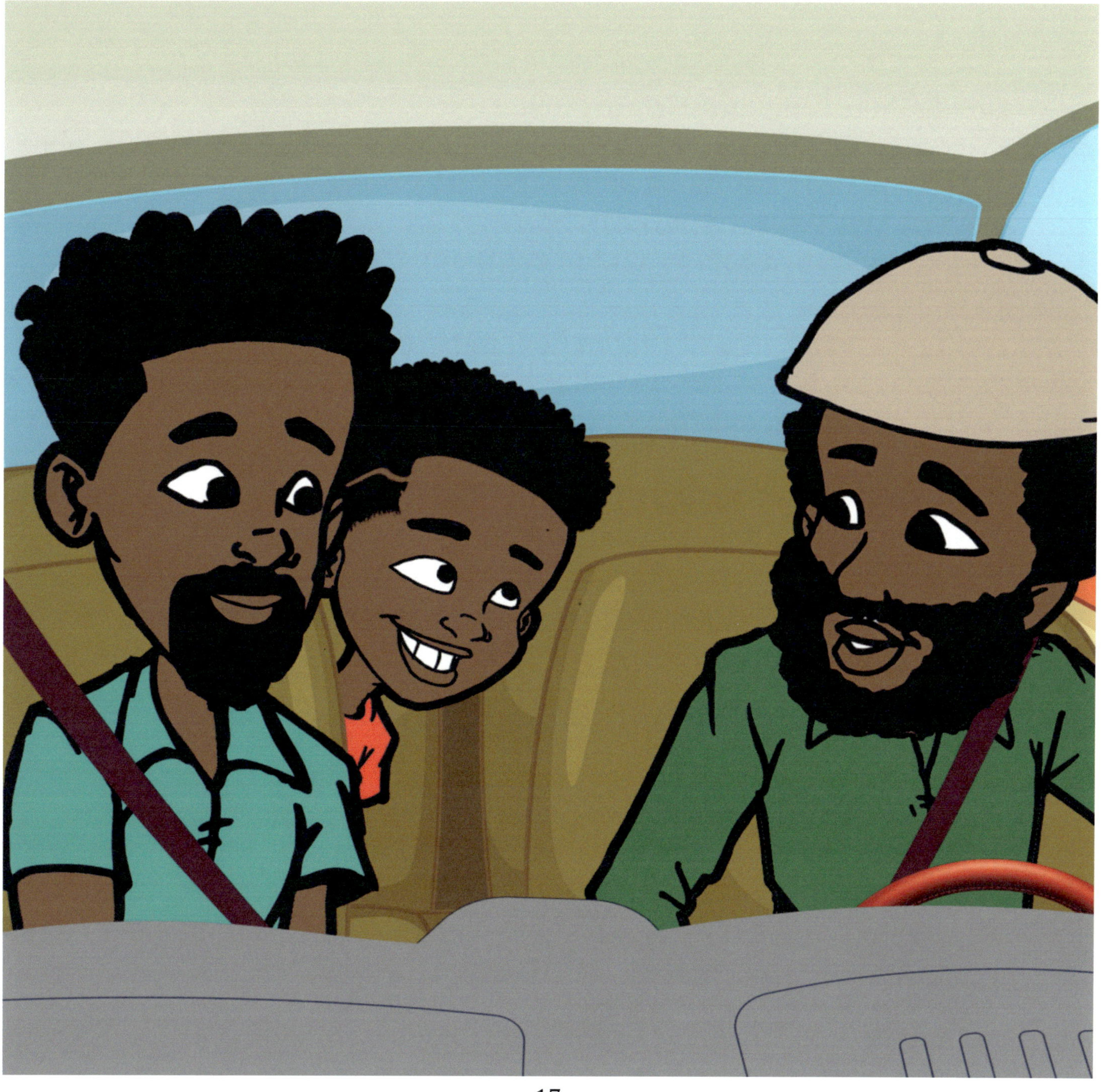

Whole Sale- Wholesaling real estate is when a real estate wholesaler puts a distressed home under contract with the intent to assign that contract to another buyer. The wholesaler doesn't plan on fixing up or selling the property. Instead, they market the home to potential buyers for a higher price than they have the property under contract for.

Fix and Flip- Fix and Flip in real estate refers to buying a property to sell it for an immediate profit rather than keep it for long-term appreciation.

Buy and Hold- Buy and hold real estate is a long-term investment strategy where an investor purchases a property and holds on to it for an extended time. The owner typically intends to sell it down the line but will rent out the property until then to help with buy and hold real estate financing.

BRRRR Strategy- The BRRRR method describes a strategy and framework used by investors who want to "buy, rehab, rent, refinance, repeat," and generate passive returns over time. This acronym indicates the steps to be executed in the correct order in which they appear.

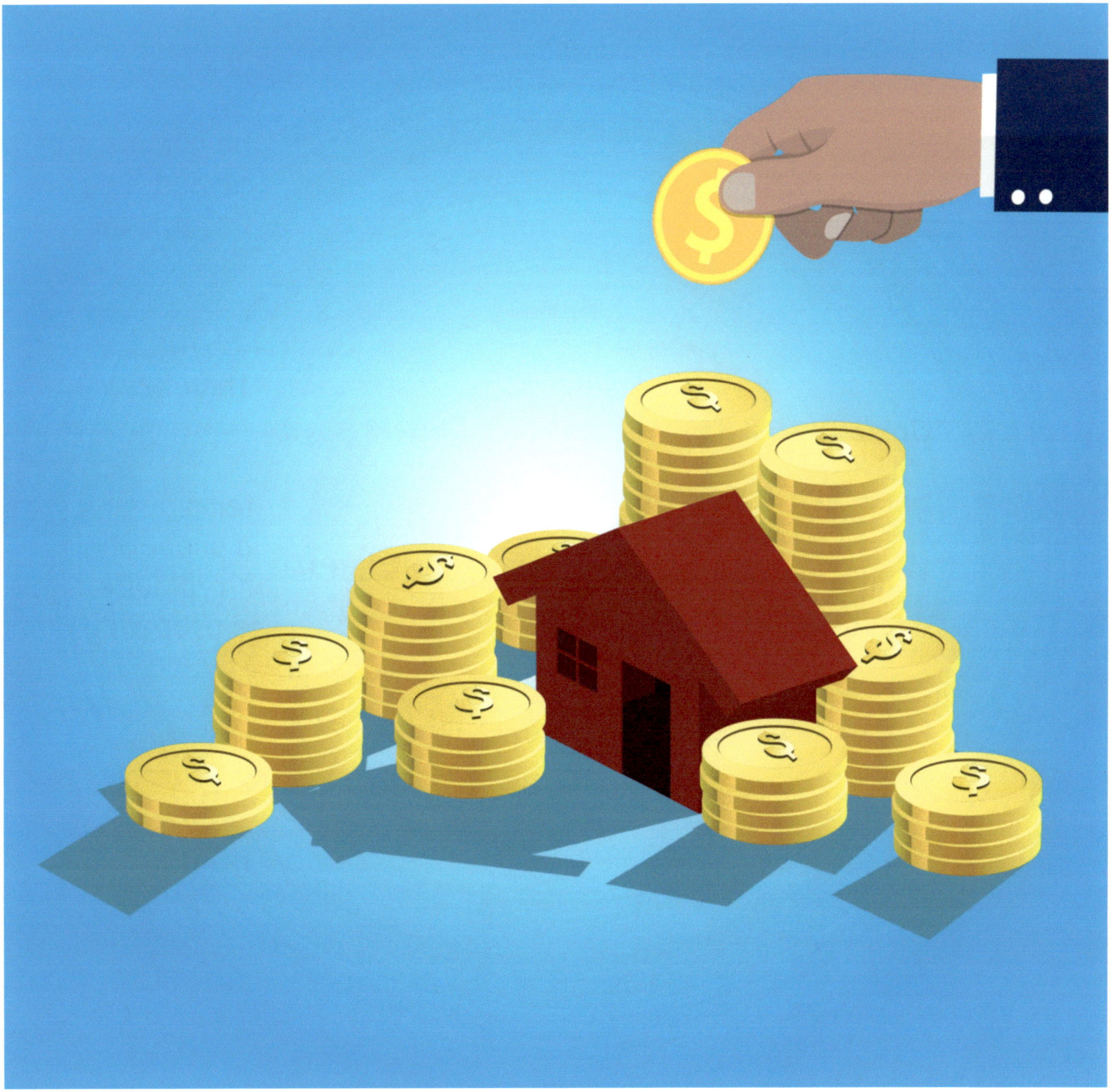

"Uncle Dre, I have a question," Robert says.

"Sure, ask away." Uncle Dre says.

"You mentioned the strategies, but what are common ways to make money in Real Estate?" Robert asks.

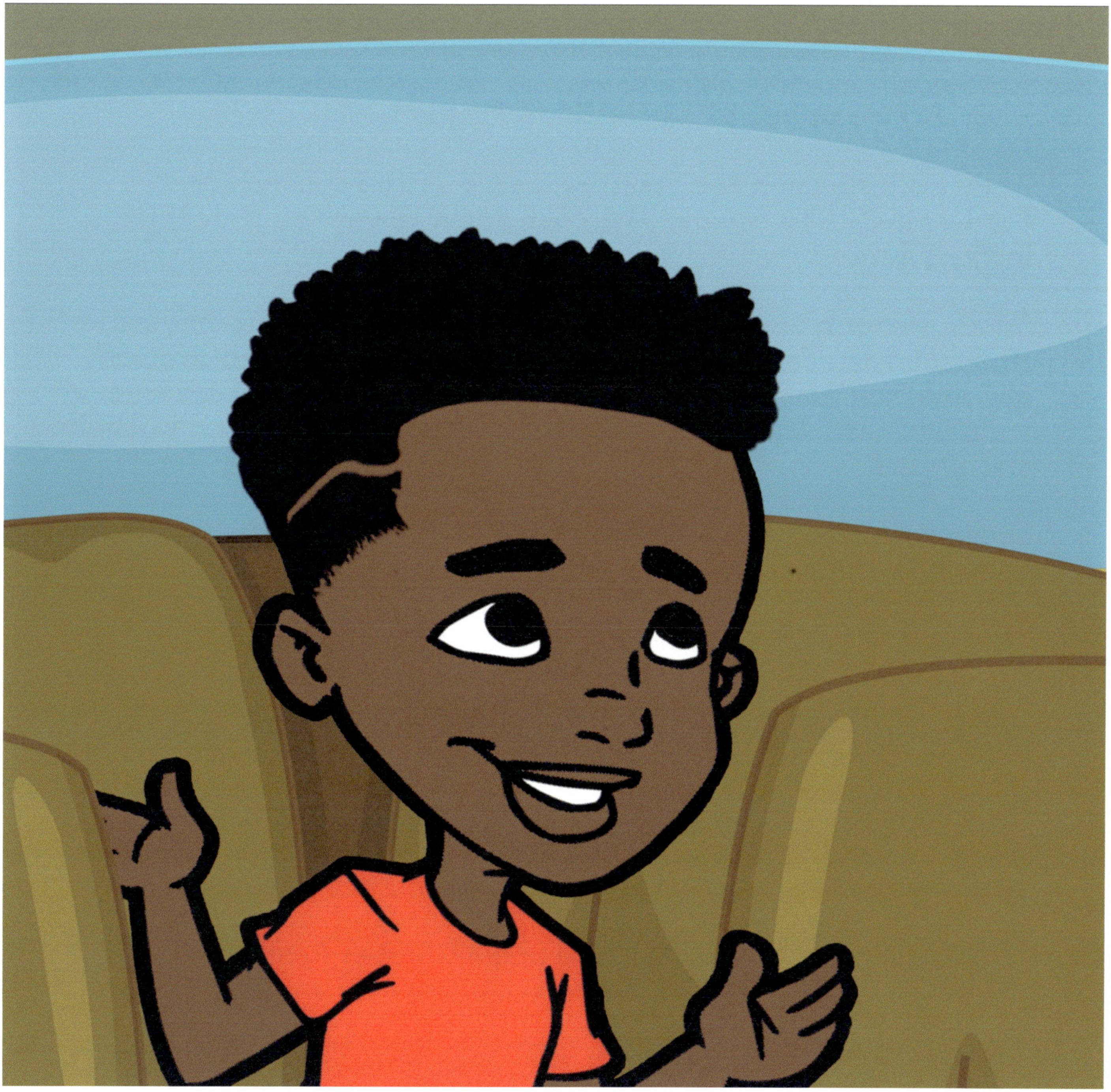

They Arrive at one of Uncle Dre's Properties.

They walk through the front and stop in the common area for Uncle Dre to remove the cash from the vending machine in the lobby.

"Well, Robert, there are four main ways. They are Real Estate Appreciation, Cash Flow Income, Real Estate Related Income, and another way is Ancillary Real Estate Investment Income, such as these vending machines and that coin-operated washers and dryers."

Uncle Dre says as he unloads the cash from the vending machine and while pointing to the laundry area.

"Ok, cool. It's all starting to come together." Robert says.

"Hey, Uncle Dre, how did you get started in Real Estate anyway." Robert's Father asks.

"It's funny you ask; I got introduced to Real Estate by being an Agent, and from there, I went to wholesaling and," Uncle Dre says before he is interrupted by Robert.

"Uncle Dre, what is wholesaling again?" Robert asks.

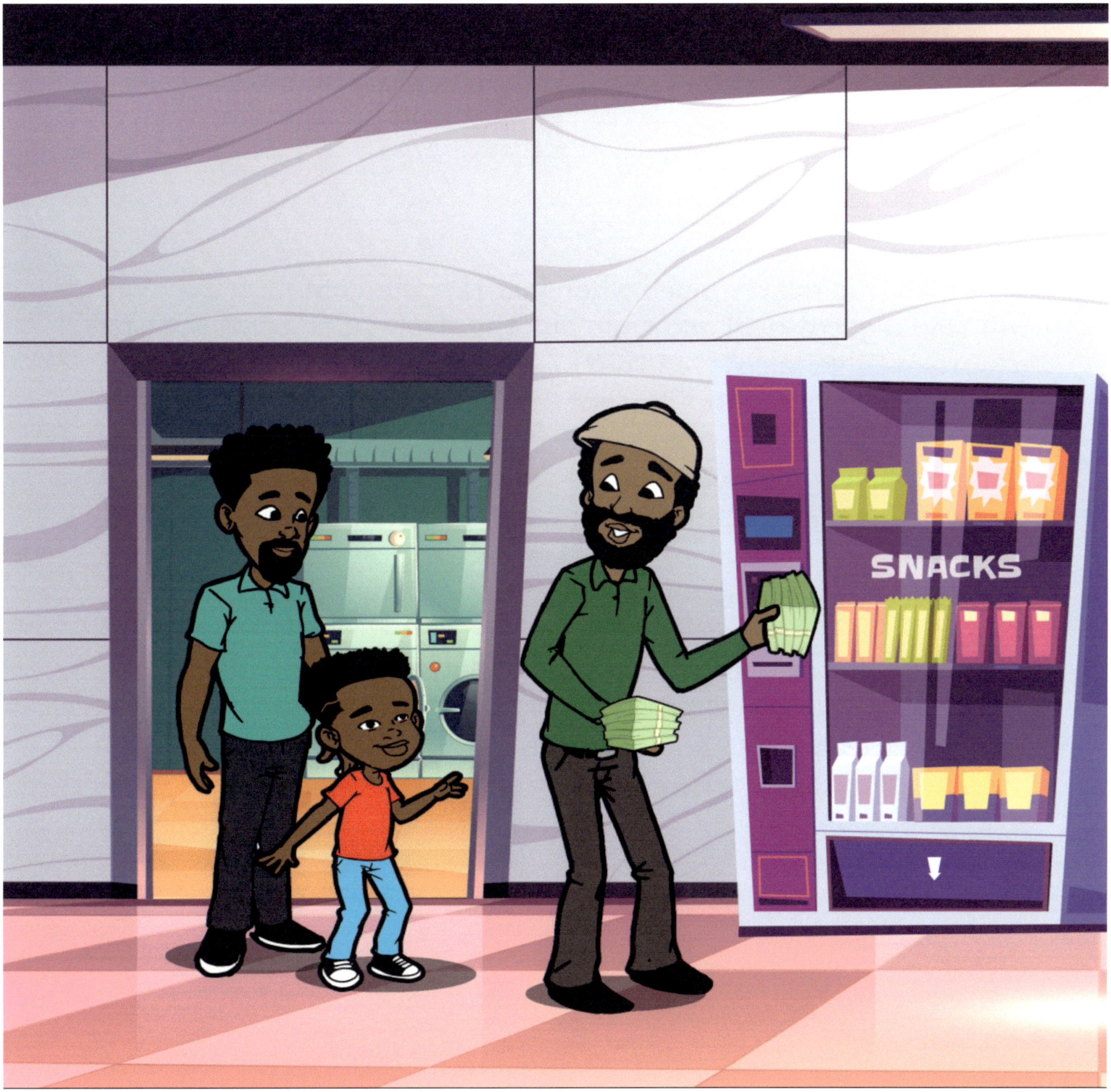
SNACKS

"Well, that is pretty much when you flip the contract. I will find a great deal and then put the deal under contract with a motivated seller. After that, I will find an ideal cash buyer and assign the contract to that buyer." Uncle Dre responds.

"After saving up enough capital from wholesaling, I went on to Fixing and Flipping Properties." Uncle Dre says.

"Is that what you and my dad are doing today?" Robert asks.

"Well, kind of. Today we will be looking for our next deal to fix and flip. So I guess you can say we are starting the process." Uncle Dre responds.

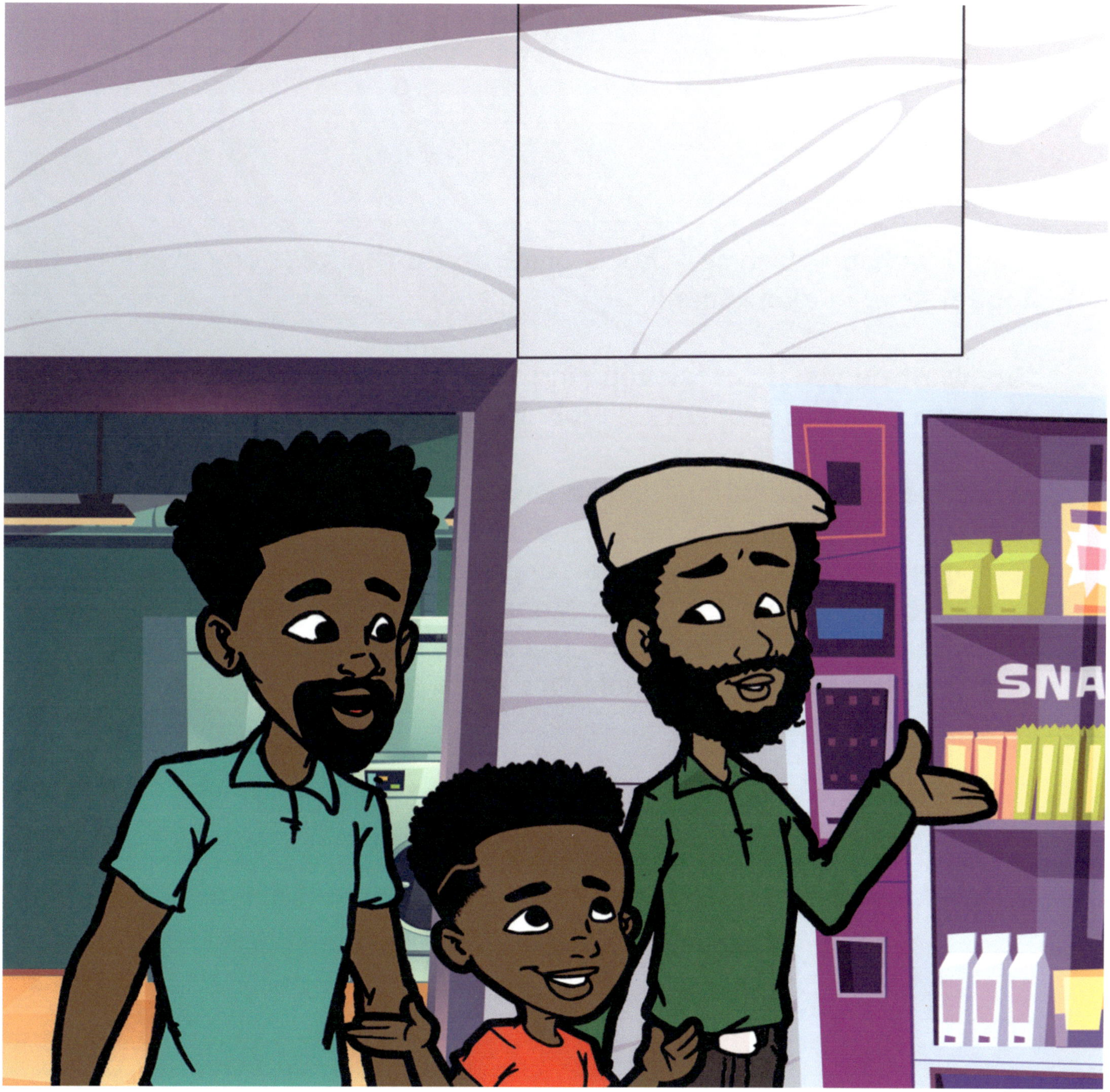
SNA

"Yay! I'm happy I came. This is going to be the best day ever!" Robert says in excitement.

"So, what do you do after you find the property? Or how do you even find the property."- Robert asks.

"That's a great question." Uncle Dre says.

"I'm going to run to the mailbox and pick up some of these rent checks, and I'll be right back. When I return, we will check out a potential property, but while I'm gone, I'll let your father answer that one." Uncle Dre adds.

Uncle Dre leaves the two and heads to the mailboxes.

27

"You see, son, Uncle Dre and I used to send mailers and postcards. We even cold call homeowners after encountering a distressed property or noticing a property entering a pre-foreclosure." Robert's father says.

"But now neither of us has the time to devote that much work, so now we just rely on local investment-friendly Real Estate agents to send us deals." Robert's father continues.

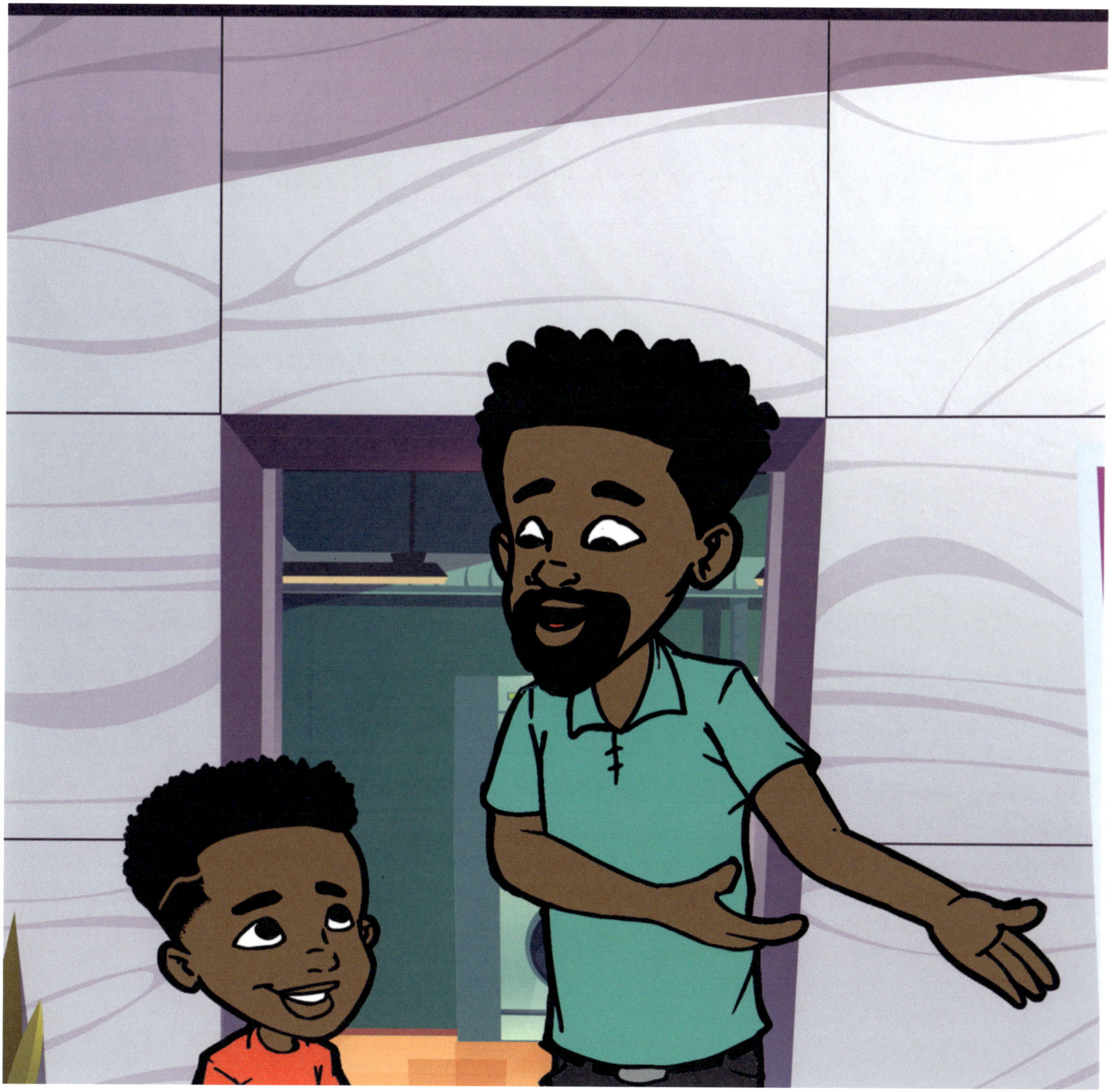

Distressed- Relating to, or experiencing economic decline or difficulty.

Acronym- A word (such as NATO, radar, or laser) formed from the initial letter or letters of each of the successive parts or major parts of a compound term.

Pre-Foreclosure- Pre-foreclosure refers to the state of a property that is in the early stages of being repossessed due to the property owner's inability to pay an outstanding mortgage obligation.

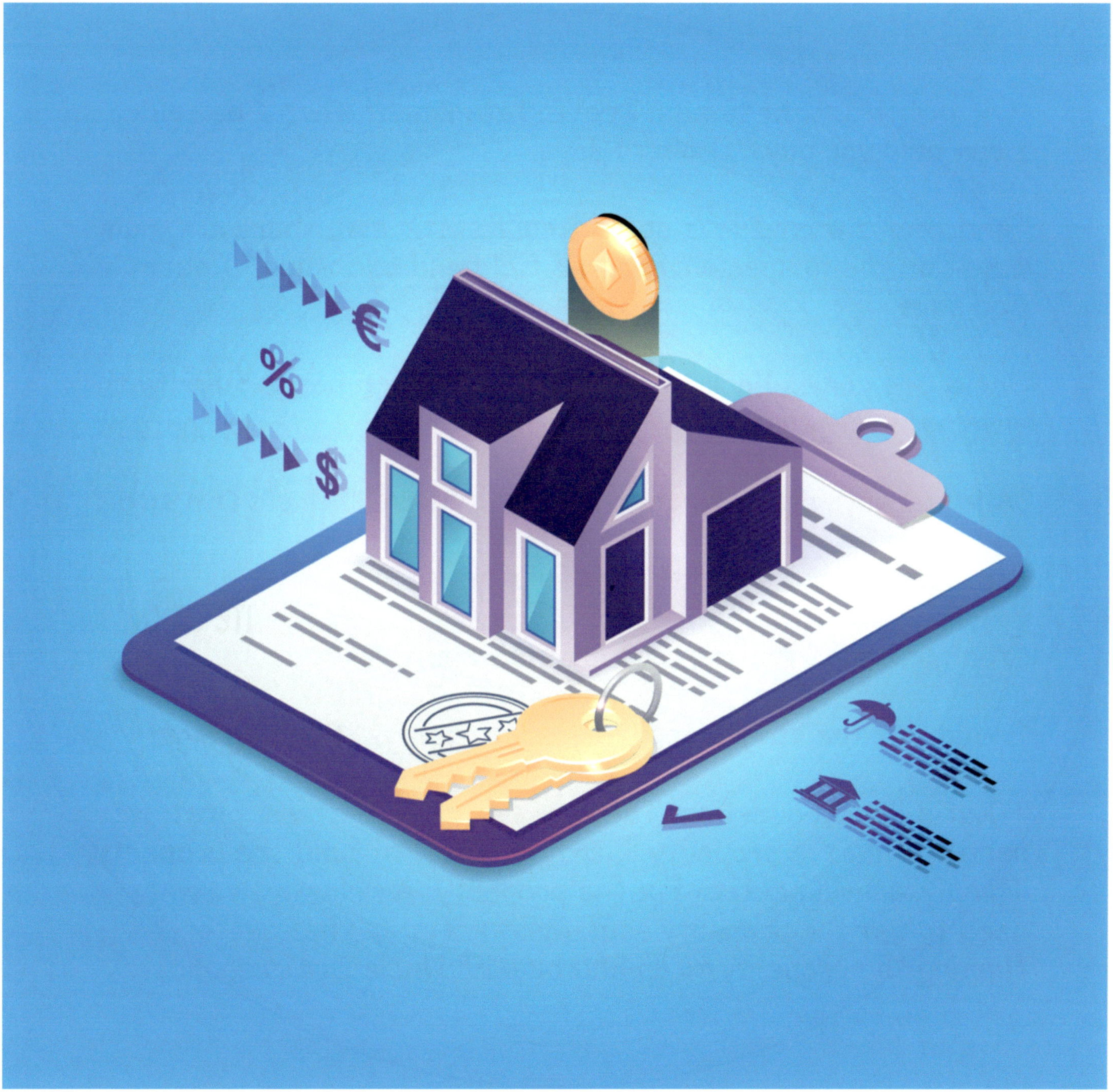

"Ok, got it. I want to be a Real Estate Agent when I get older so I can help you guys." Robert says.

"And that's what I love about Real Estate, son; there are many ways for you to specialize in the field and add value." Robert's Dad says.

Uncle Dre comes back to the group with both hands filled with envelopes (checks).

"Are you guys ready to check out this house?" Uncle Dre says.

"You know I am." Robert's Father says.

"Yeah, me too!" Robert says in excitement.

"What are the stages of fixing and Flipping?" Robert asks.

"That's a good question. They consist of four steps. First, we need to find the property. Next, we need to fund the property. Thirdly we will need to Fix the property. And lastly, we will need to get the property sold. Most refer to that as flipping the property to an end buyer." Uncle Dre responds.

33

They arrive at the property. "This looks like a good one." Robert's Father says.

"What makes a property a good one and a bad one?" Robert asks.

"Well, first thing first, the numbers always determine whether it is a good or bad deal. And by numbers, we are looking to determine if we will be able to make a profit after we calculate how much it will cost to purchase the property, fix the property, and then we have some holding costs associated with the property that we always factor in." Robert's Father answers.

"Yup, and once we calculate the numbers, we then go out and assess the property, like we are doing now. And we are looking to see if there are any structural and or foundational damages. We also like to look at the neighborhood." Uncle Dre adds.

35

"Ok, I see. And Dad, when you say you look at the numbers, what exactly are you using to determine your numbers." Robert asks.

"Well, son, first we want to look at the Purchase Price, Then we give a brief estimate of repair cost, and for that, we usually go by $60 per square foot for existing properties and $100 per square foot for new construction. And after that, we determine the ARV, which stands for After Repair Value, and that is basically how much the house will sell once it is beautiful and all fixed up." Robert's Father responds.

The group walks around the property.

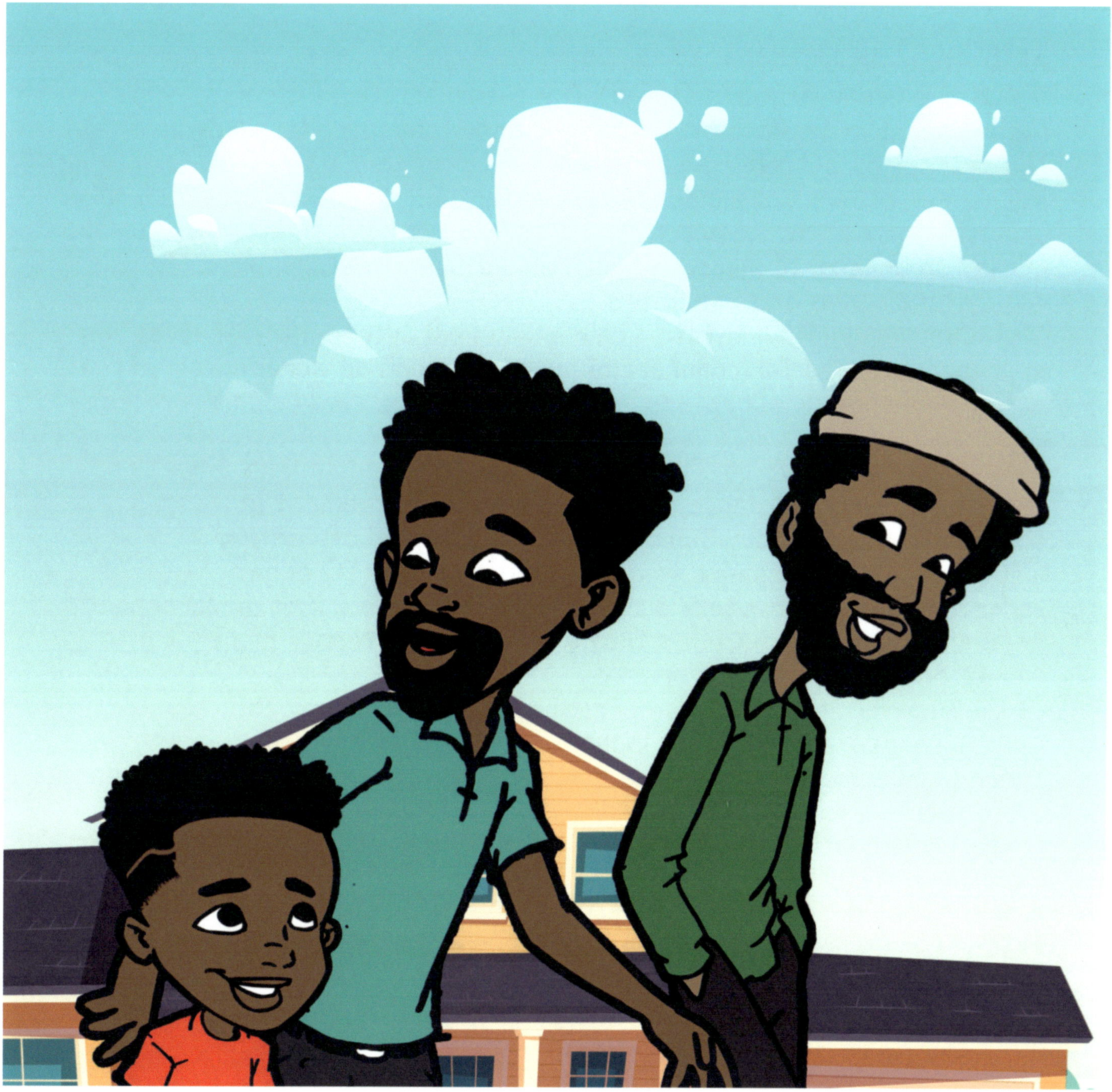

ARV-After Repair Value- Market Rate of Property after being renovated.
MAO-Maximum Available Offer- The Maximum Amount one offers.
CMA-Comparative Market Analysis- Comparative market analysis is the process of determining an investment property's value by comparing it to other properties similar in size, amenities, etc. Comparative market analysis takes both the property itself into consideration, as well as the market in general to measure this, real estate investors use different real estate comps and indicators.
CRE-Commercial Real Estate-Commercial real estate involves investing in properties used for commercial purposes, such as warehouses, offices, hotels, malls, medical centers, multi-family properties (5 units or more), etc.
FMV-Fair Market Value-The value both buyers and sellers agree upon.
L/O-Lease Option-A lease option is a type of agreement in which a tenant is allowed to buy a property after a period of renting it.
RTO-Rent to Own-Similar to a lease option, the RTO allows the tenant to buy the property during the rental period. The difference between the L/O and RTO is that RTO gives the tenant more time to secure payment for the property.
REIT-Real Estate Investment Trust- This is a company that finances, owns, manages, and operates income-producing investment properties. Individual real estate investors can invest their money in a REIT and typically receive dividends based on their cash investment.
CLSD-Closed, or Sold Listing. The property has become under contract.
OO-Owner Occupied- Owner occupied means that the owner of the property resides in it.
NOO-Non-Owner occupied- This means that the owner of the property does not reside in it when it's rented or sold, although the term is most commonly used for apartment buildings.

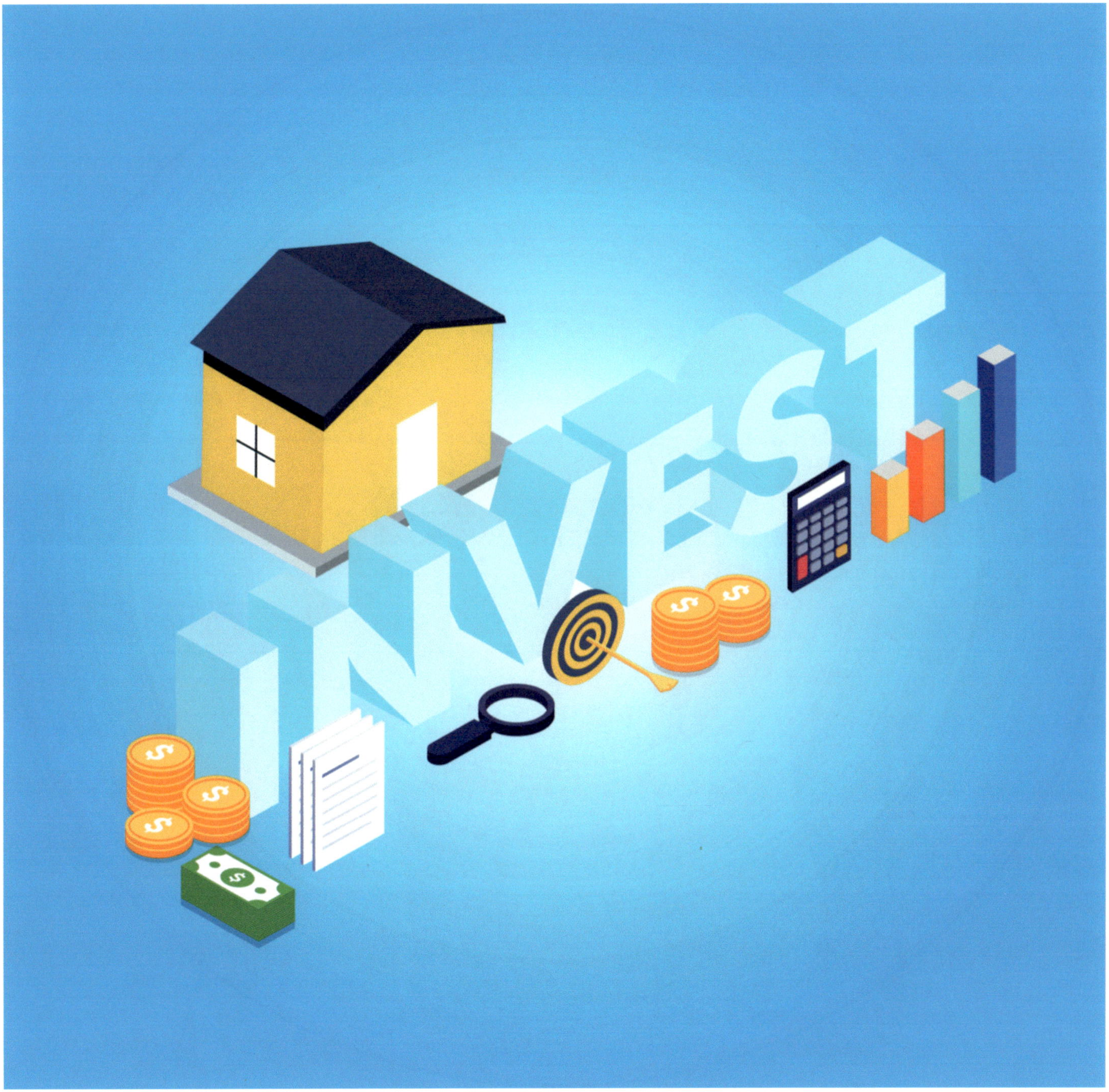
INVEST

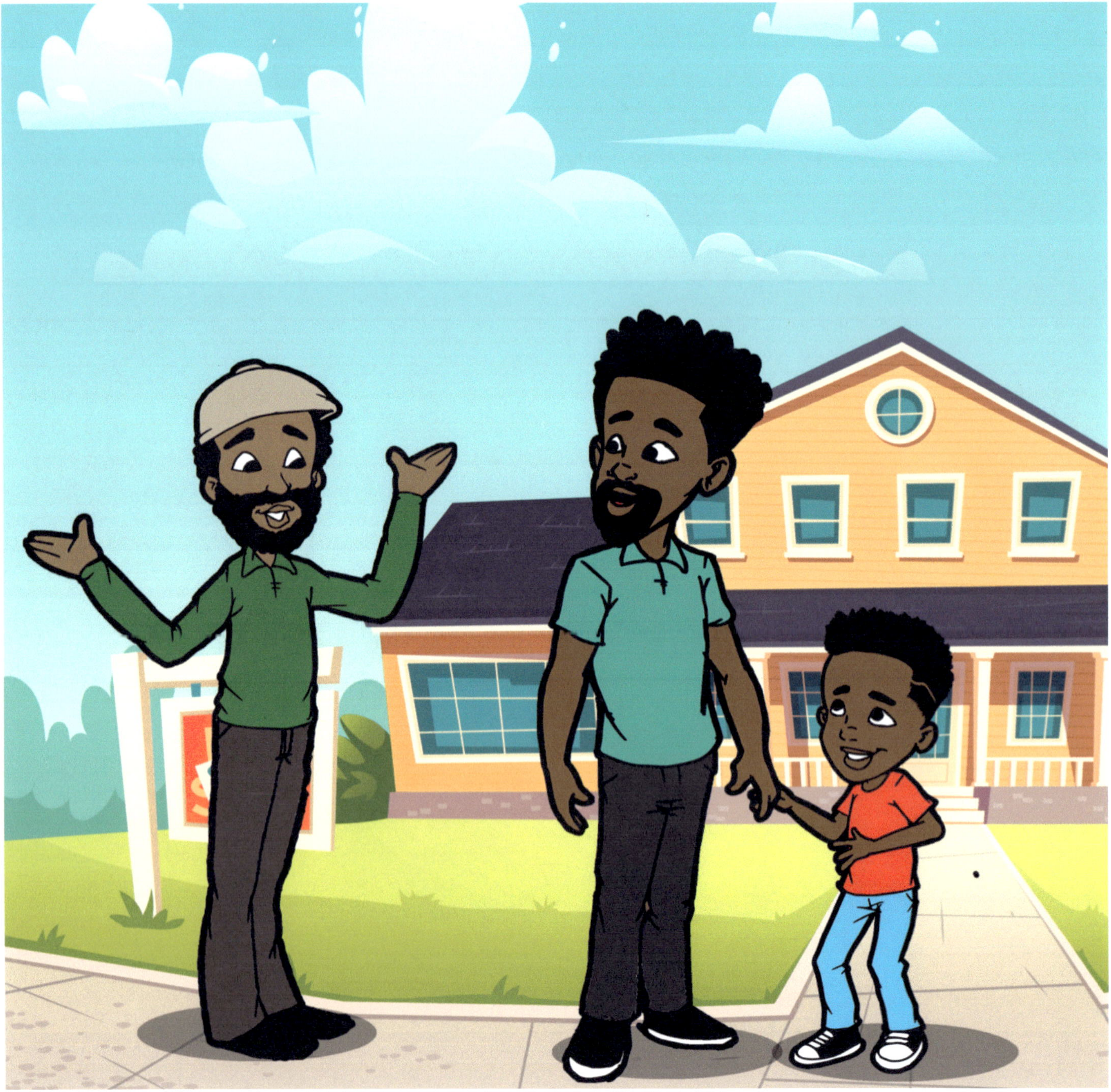

"And after you find the property, you guys just start fixing it up," Robert asks.

"We wish." Uncle Dre says as both he and Robert's Father laughs.

"Next, we need to find funding for the deal," Uncle Dre says.

"Funding? What are ways to fund it," Robert asks.

"Well, there are few ways. The most common way is by way of loan, by either using a Conventional Loan or F.H.A loan and F.H.A. stands for Federal Housing Authority. You also have Private Money, and there is also Hard Money," Uncle Dre says.

"There are many other ways, such as Subject-to, which is similar to seller financing, H.E.L.O.C which stands for Home Equity Line of Credit, V.A loans which stand for Veteran Affairs, and many others, but I don't want to confuse you today, so I'll keep it brief with the four I mentioned prior," Uncle Dre says.

Conventional Loans-A conventional loan is the most common type of mortgage. You provide a down payment and the bank gives you the rest of the money in exchange for a lien on the property secured by a mortgage.
Federal Housing Authority (FHA) Loans-FHA loans are government sponsored loans that incentivize people to purchase a home by offering a borrowing option in which the buyer needs to put down only 3.5%.
203(k) Loan-The 203(k) loan is similar to an FHA loan in that it's geared more toward homeowners than investors. It is an owner-occupied, 3.5% down a loan that allows you to lump the rehab costs into your mortgage.
Veteran Affairs (VA) Loan-Qualifying for a VA loan is one of the great advantages of serving in the military. This loan offers no-down-payment loans to veterans, service members, and select military spouses.
Private Money-Private money is financing sourced from individual (private, rather than institutional) investors. Seeking financing from family, friends, coworkers, or people you've met at your local real estate investing meetups are all potential sources of private money.
Hard Money- Hard money is similar to private money, but instead of coming from an individual, the funding comes from a hard-money lender. The term "hard money" is fitting because the lenders use the hard asset (the property) to secure the loan.
Home Equity Line of Credit (HELOC)-A home equity line of credit, popularly known as a HELOC, is what people can use if they have already purchased a home and have some equity tied up in it.
Subject To Financing-Subject to financing is when the investor or purchaser takes rights to the title for a property while the seller's existing mortgage stays in place. In the simplest terms, the real estate deal is "subject to" the seller's mortgage financing the deal.

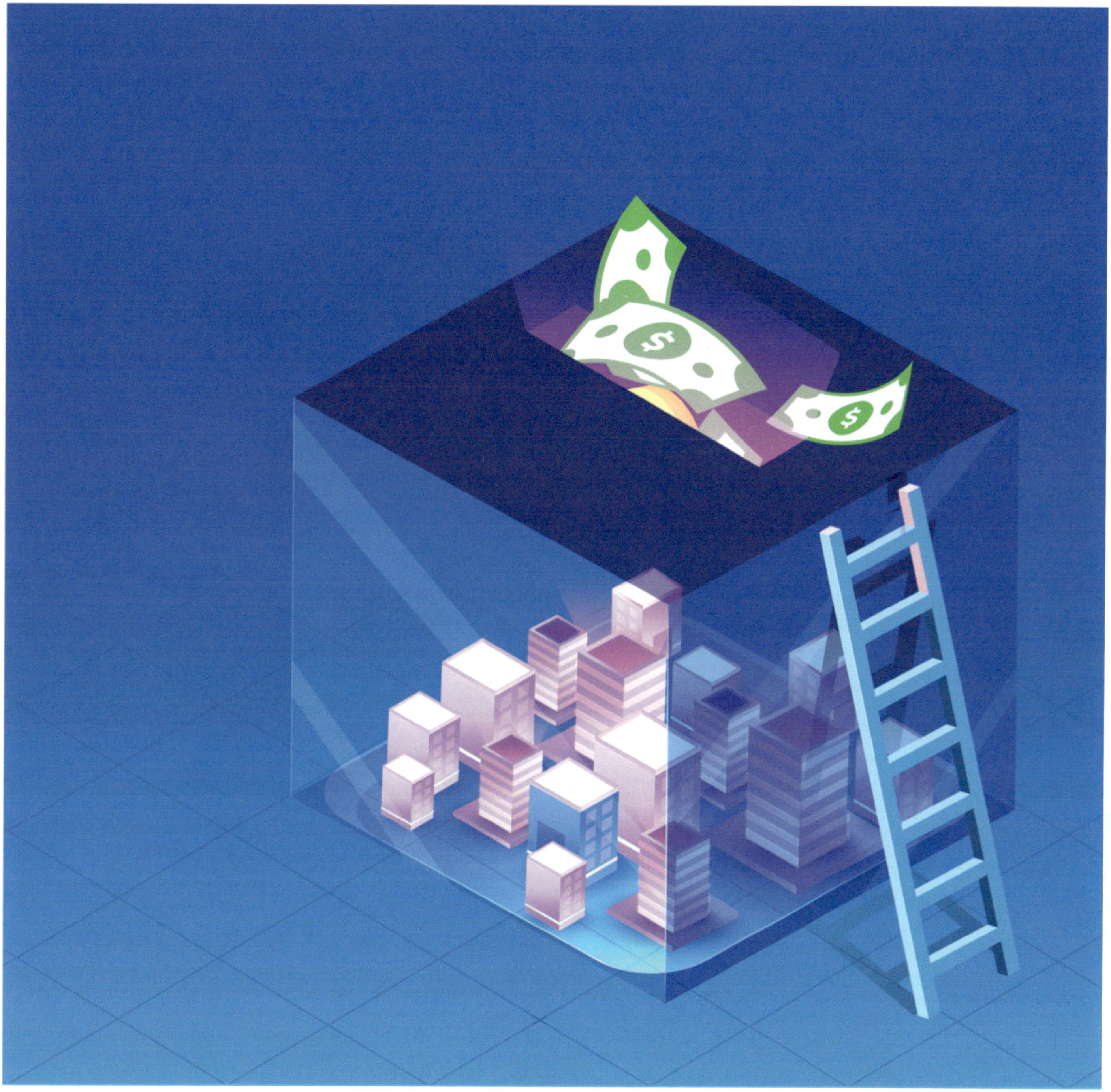

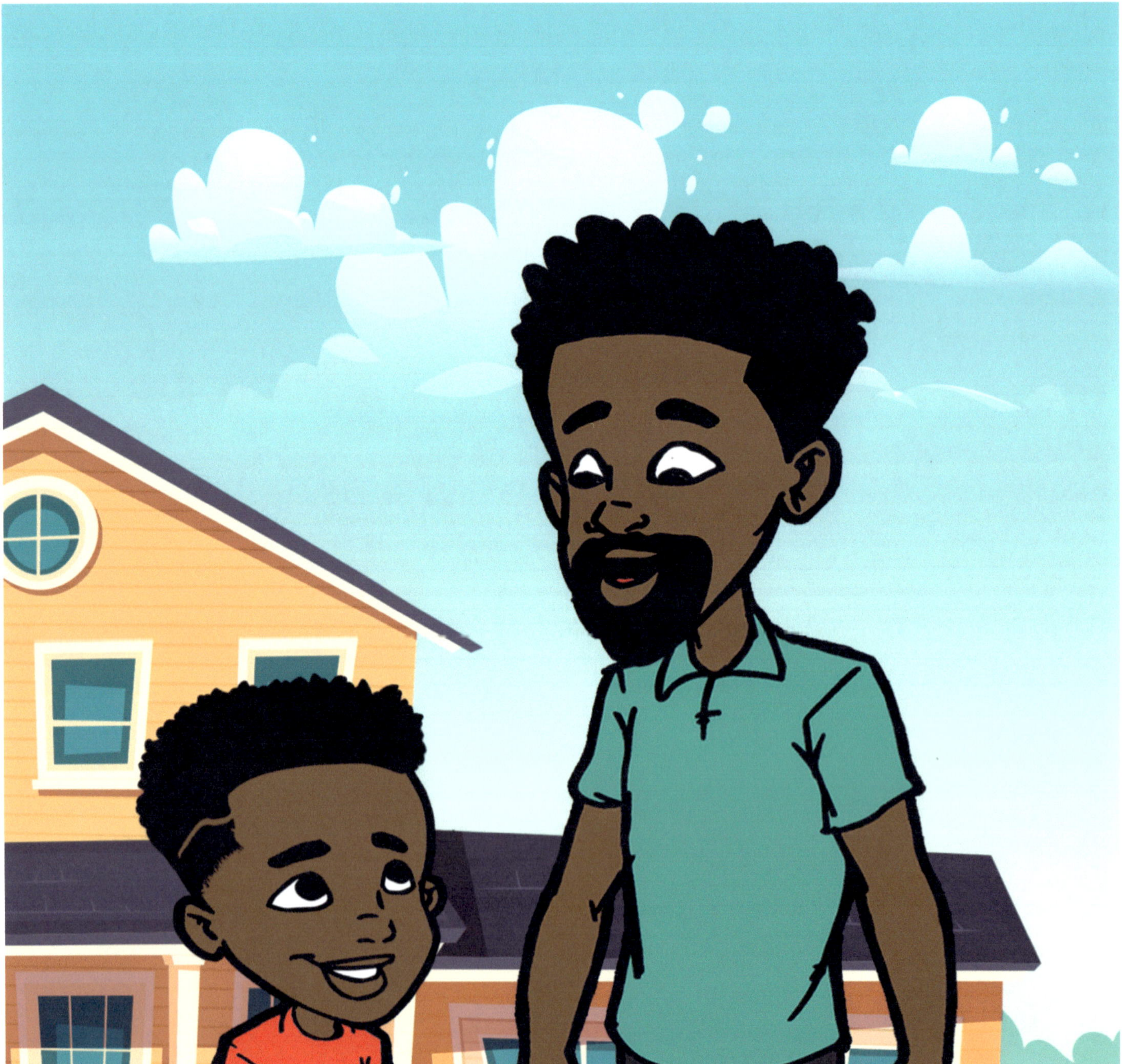

"Ok, and now do you fix the property after you fund it," Robert asked.

"That is right," Robert's father says.

"Is this a hard process," Robert asked.

"It can be if you don't know what you are doing. You see the the hardest part about fixing the property is finding the right contractors, and Uncle Dre and I have a rigorous vetting the process that we do for each deal when it comes to finding the right contractors," Robert's Dad adds.

"I see. I don't know about you two, but this information has increased my appetite. Is it lunch yet? Robert asks.

Rigorous-Characterized by or adhering to strict standards or methods; exacting and thorough.

Vetting-The process of performing a background check on someone before offering them employment, conferring an award, or doing fact-checking before making any decision.

Contractor-One that contracts or is a party to a contract such as:
a: one that contracts to perform work or provide supplies.
b: one that contracts to erect build**ings.**

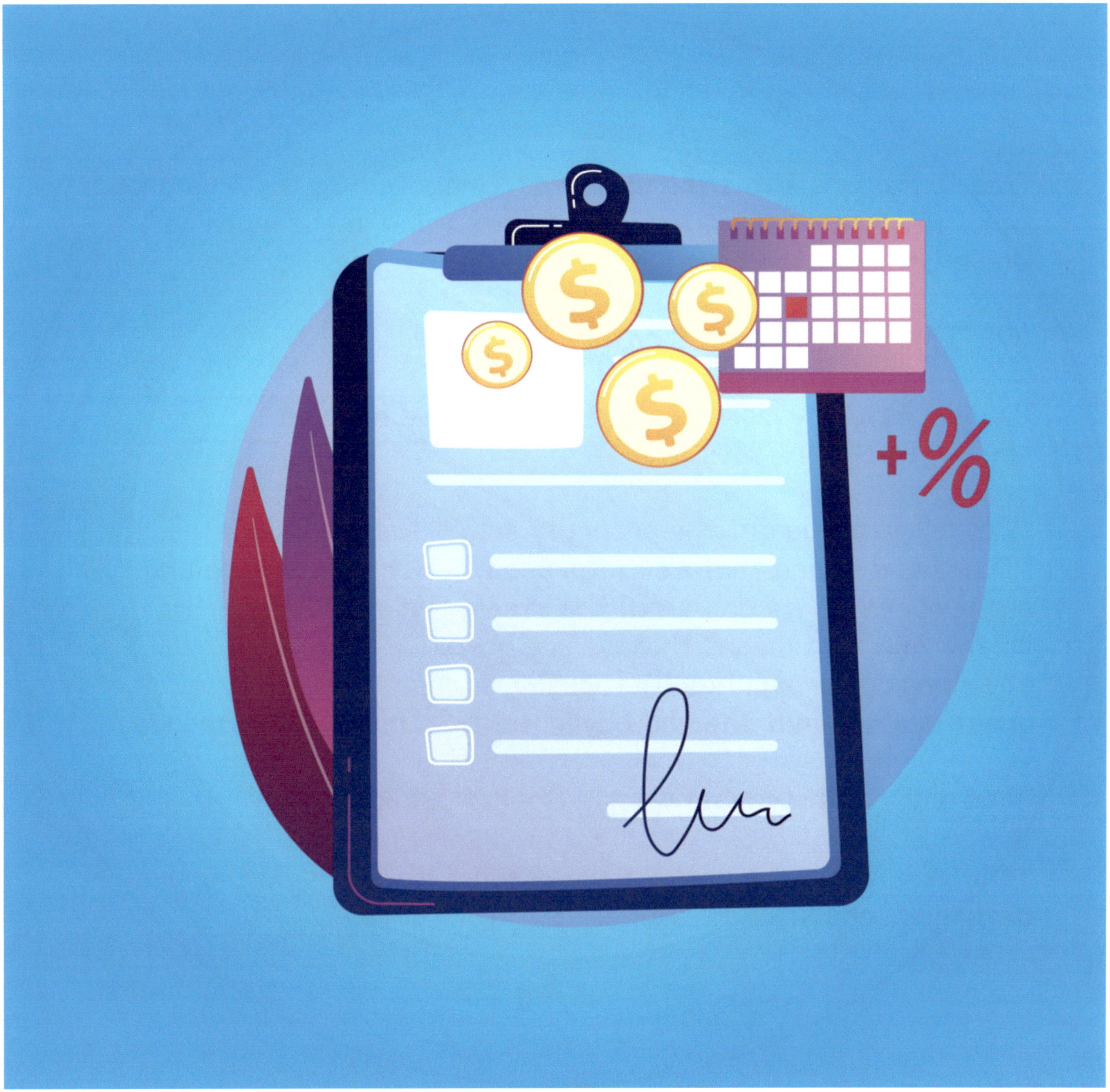

"Yes, I thought I was the only one." Uncle Dre says. "This property looks good. Let's submit an offer first thing in the morning." Uncle Dre says to Robert's Father.

"Ok, I'm on it." Robert's Father Responds.

"Do you have any more questions before we head to lunch?" Uncle Dre says.

"Yes, How do you get the property sold?" Robert asks. "There is a saying that we often use when it comes to selling our properties: we don't sell the steak. We sell the sizzle. And that means that we are great at selling our properties by focusing a great deal on what the end buyer wants," Uncle Dre responds.

"And what do they most want?" Robert asked.

"The main things we noticed that people look at is curb appeal, bathroom, and kitchen." Robert's Father says.

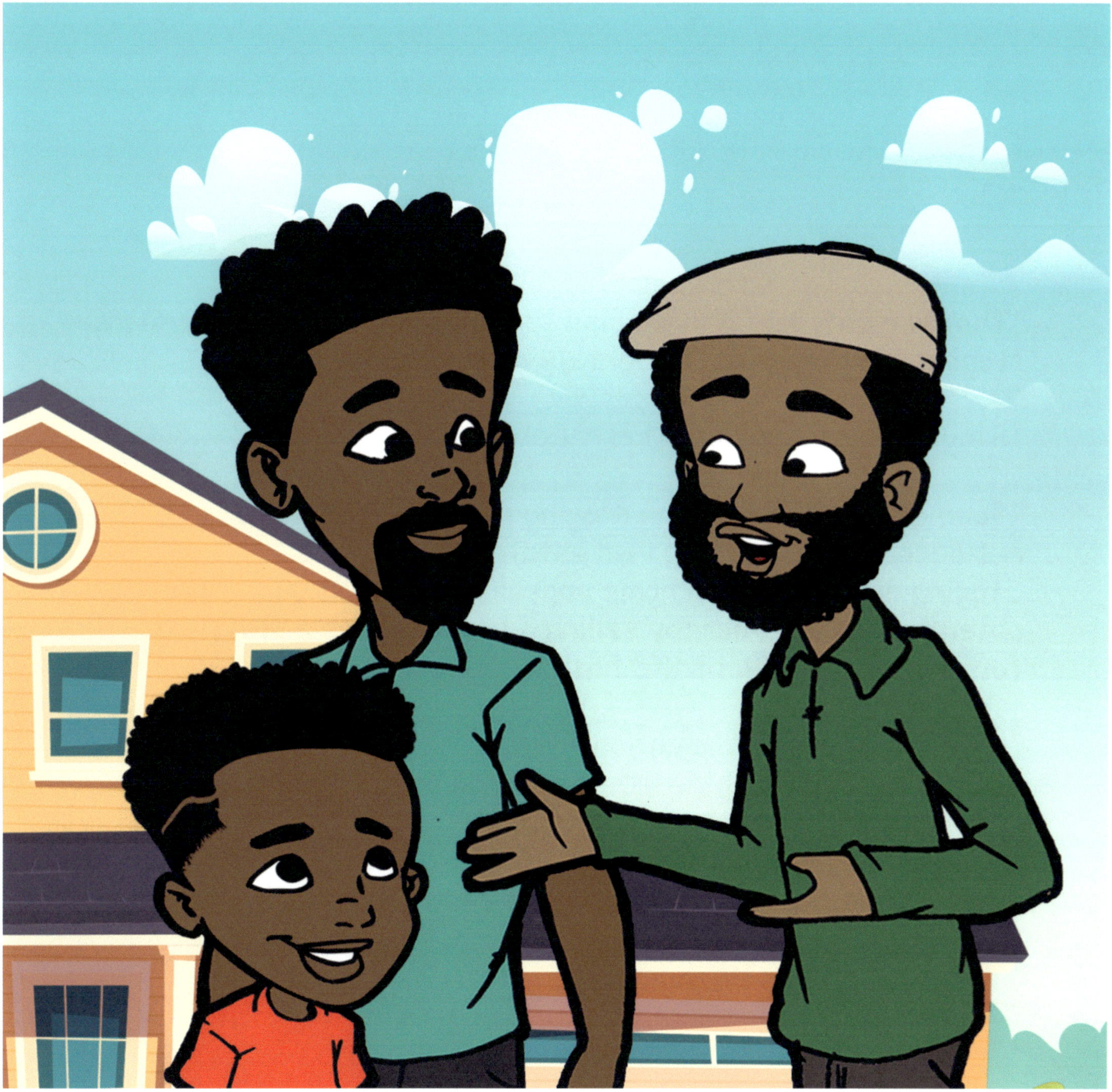

"That is right, son. And we also spend a lot of time and resources staging the property." Robert's Father says.

"Staging? What is that, Dad?" Robert asks.

"Good question, son. Home staging prepares a private residence for sale in the real estate marketplace. Staging aims to make a home appealing to the most potential buyers, thereby selling a property more swiftly and for more money." Robert's Father responds.

"And don't forget to mention the techniques." Uncle Dre adds.

"Techniques?" Robert says, confused.

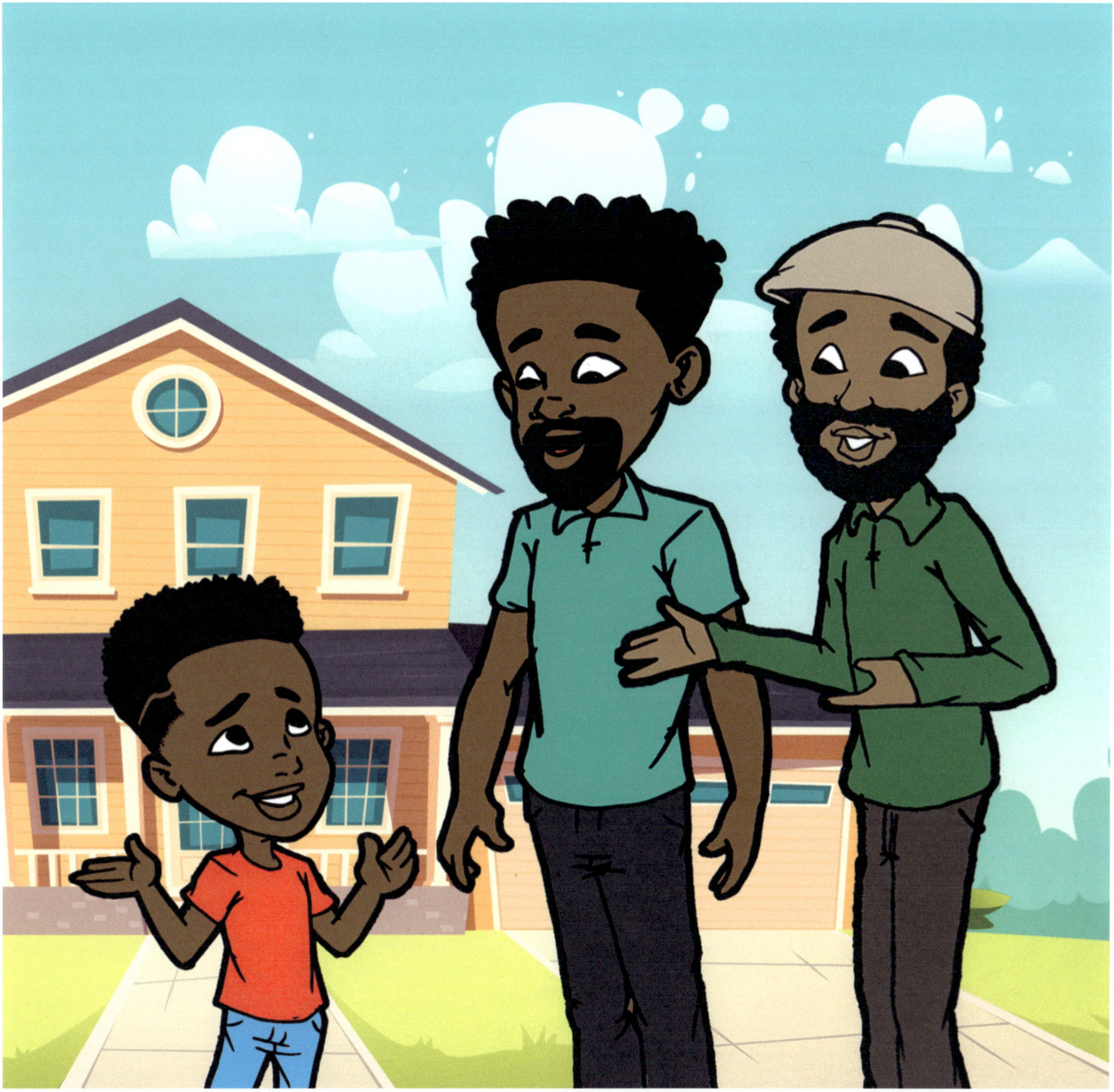

"Yes, Staging techniques focus on improving a property's appeal by ensuring it is a welcoming, attractive product that any buyer can see himself/herself living in and, thus, desire to purchase." Uncle Dre says.

"Some techniques that your father and I use include art, painting, accessories, lights, greenery, and carpet to stage the home to give potential buyers a more attractive first impression of the property." Uncle Dre continues.

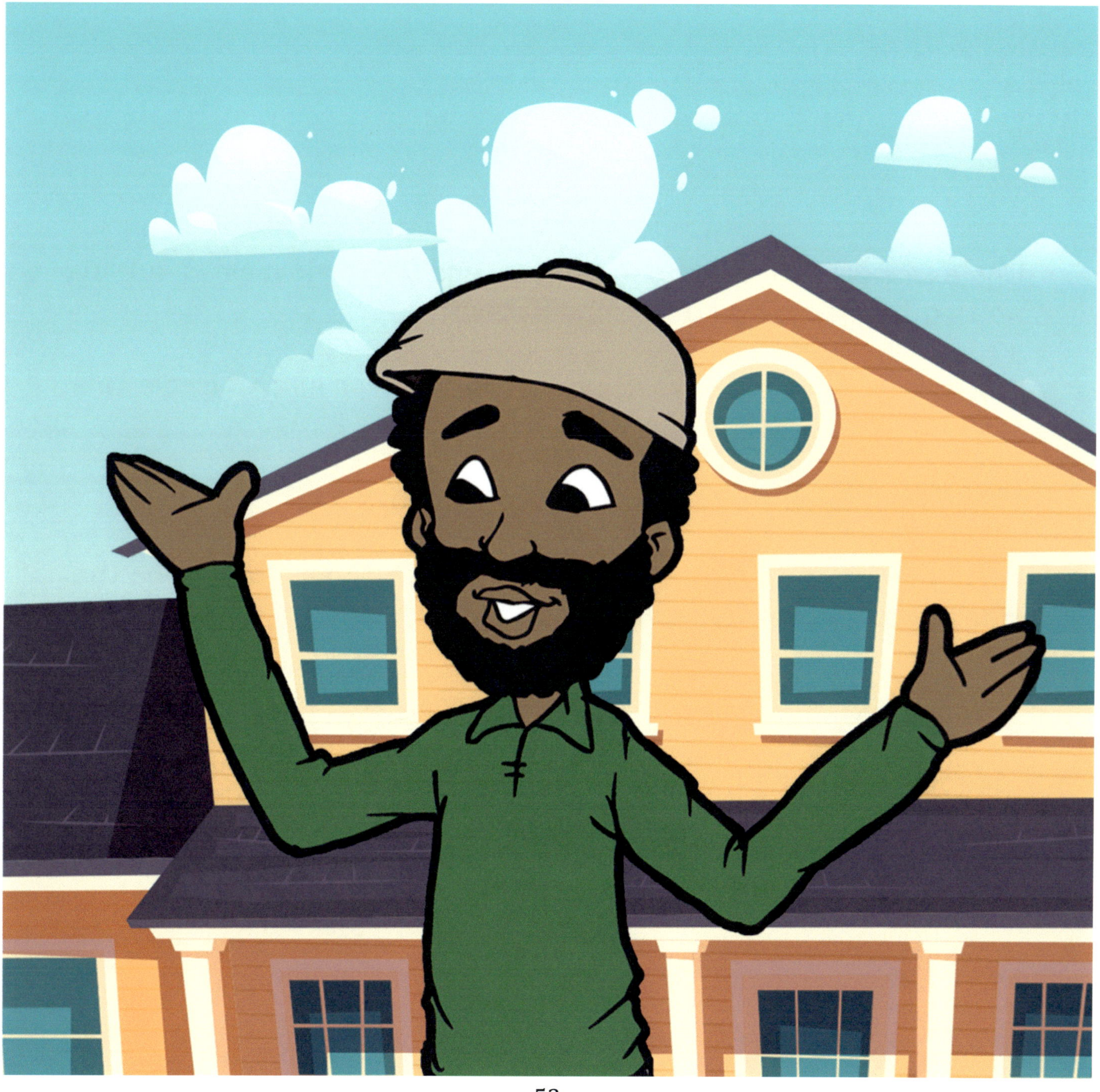

Uncle Dre arrives at Robert's house, and Robert's mom is outside waiting for Robert's Father and Robert.

"Looks like I got you guys home just in time for lunch." Uncle Dre says

"Thank you so much, Uncle Dre."- Robert says.

"Yea, thanks again for taking the time and bringing Robert on the ride along."- Robert's father says.

"Anytime." Uncle Dre says.

"I can't wait to play The Real Estate Game at school tomorrow. I know I'm going to win!" Robert says as he runs into the house.

THE END.

55

References

McElroy, K. (2004): *The ABCs of Real Estate Investing: The Secrets of Finding Hidden Profits Most Investors Miss.*. Dallas, TX: BenBella Books.

Gallinelli, F (2003): *What Every Real Estate Investor Needs to Know About Cash Flow... And 36 Other Key Financial Measures, Updated Edition.* Los Angeles, CA: California Press.

Scott, J. (2013): The Book on Estimating Rehab Costs. New York City, NY: Chronicle Books.

Turner, B. (2018): How to Invest in Real Estate: The Ultimate Beginner's Guide. New York City, NY: Avery Trade.

Scott, C. (2017): The Book on Negotiating Real Estate. New York City, NY: Penguin Press

Tyson, E. (2007): Real Estate Investing For Dummies. Nashville, TN: Integrative Nutrition Publishing.

Blank, M. (2018): Financial Freedom with Real Estate Investing. New York City, NY: Penguin.

Terms of Use

All use of the *Robert's Real Estate Game book*, accessible at www.childrentowealth.com and related subdomains (collectively, the "Web site") is subject to the following terms and conditions and our Privacy Policy all of which are deemed a part of and included within these terms and conditions (collectively, the "Terms"). By accessing the book you are acknowledging that you have read, understand, and agree to be bound by these Terms.

These Terms represent a binding contract between you and *Mudaris LLC* (and any of their respective principals, officers, shareholders, members, employees or agents are herein collectively referred to as *"Children To Wealth"* or "we"). These Terms are in addition to any other agreements between you and Mudaris LLC. If you do not agree with any of these terms and conditions, please do not use this book.

Mudaris LLC reserves the right to change, modify, add or remove portions of these Terms at any time for any reason. Such changes shall be effective immediately upon posting. You acknowledge by accessing our book after we have posted changes to this Agreement that you are agreeing to these Terms as modified.

TRADEMARKS, COPYRIGHTS AND OTHER INTELLECTUAL PROPERTY

The content contained in the book is owned, licensed or otherwise lawfully used by *Mudaris LLC* and is protected by applicable copyrights, trademarks, service marks, and/or other intellectual property rights. Mudaris LLC hereby grants you access to its original content pursuant to a Creative Commons Attribution-Noncommercial-ShareAlike License, the terms of which are accessible at: http://creativecommons.org/licenses/by-nc-sa/3.0/legalcode. *Mudaris LLC* hereby expressly reserves all rights not expressly granted in and to the book and its content.

Visit ChildrenToWealth.com and view more books that you will Enjoy!

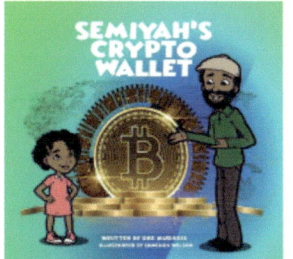

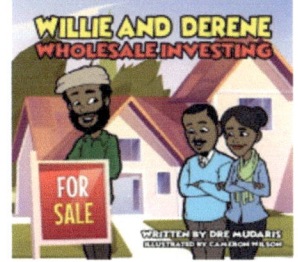

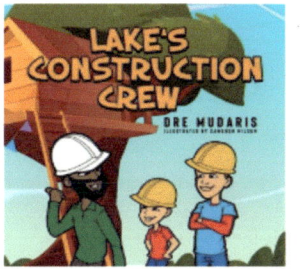

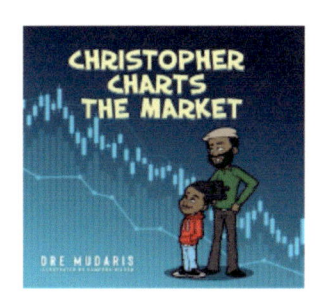

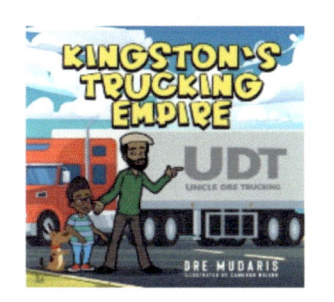

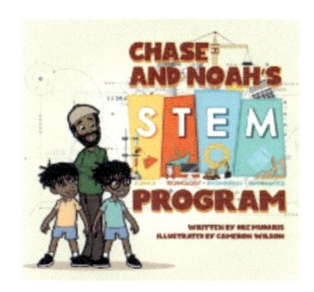

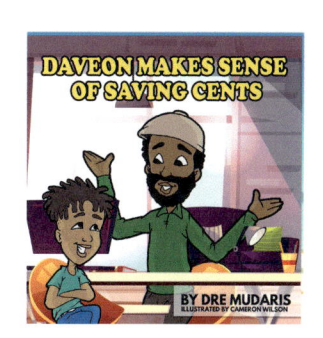

And Much More !!!

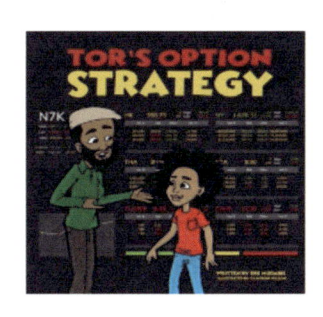

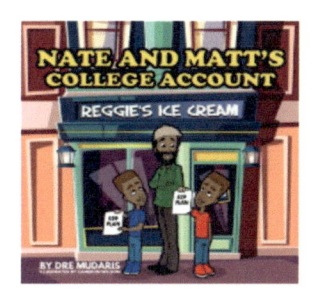

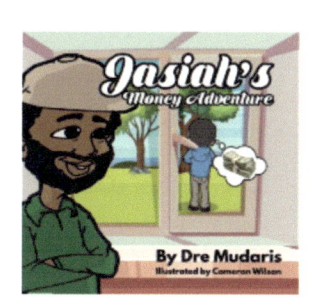

Made in the USA
Columbia, SC
12 August 2024